CW00531619

ROSES

AND HOW TO MAKE
THE MOST OF THEM

First Published 1998 by Hyndman Publishing P O Box 5017, Dunedin

ISBN 1-877168-22-X

TEXT: © Bill Ward

CONCEPT AND FORMAT: Neil Hyndman

RESEARCH AND IDEAS: Bill Ward and Mark Slattery

LAYOUT AND DESIGN: Di Leva Graphic Design

PHOTOGRAPHY: Mark Hamilton

ILLUSTRATIONS: Sheila Boerkamp

PRINTING: Tablet Colour Print

1st Reprint May 1999

All rights reserved. No part of this publication is to be produced, stored in a retrieval system, or transmitted in any form or by means electronic, mechanical, or photocopying without prior written permission of the publisher.

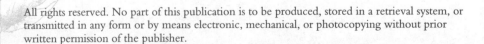

Contents

Introduction

Roses are often referred to as the "Queen of Flowers". They were popular in the ancient civilisations of Egypt, Rome and Greece. Over the years they have captivated all who come into contact with them.

There is no secret to good rose growing. Given the right conditions, roses will respond by producing abundant blooms to delight the gardener, whether experienced or a complete novice.

In today's gardens roses need not stand in gaunt isolation in a specialist rose bed, or ramble without purpose. Creating a picture postcard Garden of Eden with roses in your own garden is easy if you know how. This book provides a practical guide to how anyone, by choosing the correct roses and planting them in the right places, can easily create some of the most wonderful displays — shows that last for months and require very little care.

If your garden can grow weeds then you can grow roses. Whether you live in a city apartment or on a large estate, you can enjoy the pleasure roses bring. I share my experience on which roses have always given me success and are easy to grow.

The roses I have listed in this book are only a small selection from the world of beautiful, exciting and rewarding roses.

Once you, too, have successfully grown them you will become hooked. No doubt you will be drawn to experiment with the multitude of varieties as I have been.

Bill Ward

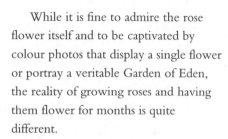

Using Roses

While it is fine to admire the rose flower itself and to be captivated by colour photos that display a single flower or portray a veritable Garden of Eden, the reality of growing roses and having them flower for months is quite different.

With the thousands of varieties available, it is fair to say many of us don't know where to begin. Having made a selection, we can often be disappointed if the rose does not live up to our expectation. Some reward their owners by flowering for only a few weeks each year. Despite this short and often beautiful display, they then sit around in the garden looking tatty for months.

To create a picture postcard display you need to know how to choose the right rose.

REPEAT VS NON REPEAT

There are many different types of roses. Some provide a short but spectacular display, but if you want to have blooms for as long as possible it is important to select a rose which has a long flowering period.

Wedding Day and Albertine are two popular non-repeat climbers, magnificent in their display over a few weeks but then leaving a barren look. Compare these with the repeat-flowering Compassion or Crepuscule, which begin flowering in early summer and bloom right through to autumn.

While Wedding Day and Albertine are both fabulous roses, I have written this book as a guide for those of us who prefer their roses to flower for months on end rather than for just a few weeks.

To ensure long displays with your roses, you need to look for roses labelled free-flowering, long-flowering, continuous, recurrent or repeat-flowering, rather than choosing those

Using Roses

continued

whose description is ambiguous or which perhaps are described as spring or summer flowering.

Descriptions such as "flowers throughout the season" can be confusing as roses labelled as such can have one glorious flush that lasts for a month and then scattered blooms for the rest of the season.

In the photos on pages 13–16 I have shown a repeat-flowering rose, The Fairy, and the many effects this rose has when used in different settings. In containers, as a climber, a standard, or, in mixed planting.

THE FAIRY

One of the world's favourite roses, The Fairy is a polyantha hybrid and bears large trusses of mid-pink blooms. It is well known for its generous blooming over a long flowering season — from late spring through to early winter.

Once you have experienced the delights of The Fairy you may never want anything else. They are hard to beat for adaptability and diversity. They always seem to be in flower and can be left to their own devices to sprawl or can be trimmed to shape to grow in tubs.

Roses that offer such a long flowering period provide the foundation for colour in your garden.

Choosing the right roses for your garden

TYPES OF ROSES

There are many types of roses, from old-fashioned varieties such as the wild roses, Gallicas, Damasks, through to the hybrids. Modern roses such as the Hybrid Tea, Floribunda and David Austin English Roses have been a boon for gardeners. Rose breeders now produce plants that are more disease-resistant and have longer flowering seasons than many of the older varieties.

Roses for the home gardener to choose:

Hybrid Tea — Undoubtedly classic. Developed for their vigour, health and disease resistance. Many have perfectly formed buds held singularly on long stems. Often fragrant, they are the classic picking rose, providing a wonderful garden display also. Words simply do not do justice to the beauty of a single flower resting in a bud vase. Its solitary appeal is often underestimated.

Floribunda — The best choice for a great show in the garden, producing a mass of colour. The blooms are borne in clusters both large and small. They flower repeatedly throughout the season and are very strong, making them less vulnerable to attack by fungal diseases.

Climbing roses — Ramblers (old-fashioned, usually flowering once) and modern climbers. Many moderns are repeat- flowering. The modern varieties have thicker canes and fewer of them, which makes them easier to train. Few people realise how effective climbing roses can be. They are excellent for disguising a stark fence line or covering a bare wall.

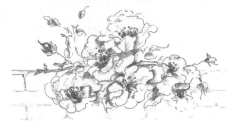

Choosing the right roses for your garden

continued

BILL'S TIP

Standards — if planted into a lawn they need a circle or square of earth at least one metre across to allow water to get to the roots (under-plant with ground-cover roses, annuals or perennials by all means). Ensure you stake standards well — special stakes are available from your garden centre.

Miniature roses/Patio roses — Miniature roses are repeat-flowering and can be fragrant too. These roses are ideal as specimens, for the smaller garden or when used in containers (they also look great when brought indoors). Miniature roses, while delicate to look at, need no special care. They are just like their big brothers and will stand up to life in the garden.

English roses — David Austin bred these and he describes them as having "form, character and growth of old roses with a repeat-flowering habit and the colour range of modern roses". Most are fragrant as well. They are adaptable and resilient — proven performers.

Old-world roses — From singles to doubles, these roses have the widest diversity of any rose group in terms of different flower forms. They are highly scented, but many do not repeat-flower and some are disease prone. Old-world roses often provide a stunning display of tomato red, orange or yellow rose hips in autumn. What a bonus!

ROSES FOR SHADY PLACES

It has become a popular notion that roses cannot be grown successfully in shady conditions. This is quite untrue. In situations where there is some filtered light and the soil is well drained, there are a number of roses that will thrive. To help with your selection, a list of shade-tolerant and shade-loving roses that are repeat-flowering can be found at the back of this book.

Choosing the right roses for your garden

continued

As a general rule, the brightly coloured roses (reds, yellows, oranges etc) need sunlight to retain their colours and are therefore unsuited to shady spots. The softer-coloured roses (pinks, whites, soft pastels) are ideally suited. Pale colours provide another advantage — their flowers work well "lightening up" otherwise dull aspects.

The Alba group of roses are ideal — free-flowering throughout the summer. An added bonus is the large hips displayed extravagantly in autumn. Windrush is a lemon-coloured English rose with a sweet scent that flowers and flowers — it is one of my personal favourites. Seafoam is my choice for a white-flowered rambler, Crepuscule for apricot.

Most of us have a shady spot or two in our garden, so why not consider growing a rose such as Windrush, Seafoam or Crepuscule there?

ROSES FOR HOT AND HUMID CONDITIONS

In warmer climates it is not important which rose you choose; it is more important that you know how to care for them.

The combination of humidity and poor air circulation leads to poor plant health and then disease. This is why many people lose their roses or have limited success. It is very important if you live in a humid climate that you spread your roses apart (1–1.5 metres to allow for good air circulation is a rule of

Choosing the right roses for your garden

continued

thumb I recommend). However, this does not mean you cannot plant other plants between your roses. Plant away to your heart's content, as long as you ensure there is good air movement through the top of the rose.

When planting roses against solid walls and fences or any other structure that restricts air movement, I recommend you set a frame such as a trellis 30-50 cm from the structure for your roses to grow on. This way they will get the air movement they need. Using chains suspended from your house for your roses to grow on is a great alternative.

Watering in hot climates is important. Roses need plenty of water (refer to the care of roses section), but take care. Watering early in the morning is best, and a Plassay drip system works wonders. Overhead watering causes problems to the foliage and buds. If they are wet and sun gets on the foliage and/or the buds they will go brown quickly. Once this happens you have the ideal breeding ground for fungus.

In very hot areas I recommend mulching. This simply means putting a protective covering over the ground around your roses. Anything like shredded newspaper, sawdust (untreated of course), bark, pea straw, or mush-room compost are ideal as mulches. Avoid using fresh lawn clippings as they will burn the feeder roots on your roses.

Before applying a mulch, water your roses thoroughly, then spread your

Choosing the right roses for your garden

continued

mulch, covering at least a metre. Apply mulch to a depth of about 5cm. Be careful not to mulch too close to the crown of your rose plant otherwise your rose will "sweat" and may defoliate. Mulching helps to keep your roses roots cool and reduces water loss.

In warmer climates, consider planting low-growing, heat-tolerant plants to assist water retention. Annuals such as alyssum, lobelia, marigolds, dianthus and violas fit the bill nicely and add fragrance to the garden. Alyssum is a good indicator plant as it wilts when the ground is dry, telling you all the plants need water.

Thyme works well as a permanent ground cover and rosemary is also a favourite. These need little water and don't compete with roses. If you are considering rosemary, the prostrate rosemary is the one to use. Its sky blue flowers and dark foliage accentuate the brighter colours of some roses.

ROSES FOR COASTAL CONDITIONS

Heavier soils are preferable for roses, although sandy soils can also give good results. When preparing your soil, regardless of type, always incorporate generous quantities of peat and compost. Their inclusion improves the water-holding capacity of the soil. A six-monthly dose of slow-release fertiliser is important as sandy soils leach rapidly.

Select a sunny open situation which is protected from strong winds. If you are near the sea, it may pay to consider putting a windbreak around the rose to keep the salt air off for the initial growing season. If planting in a windy spot, plant in groupings of three to five. Roses planted this way will give a degree of protection to one another.

Wooden fencing is ideal as a windbreak. If you want a more natural windbreak, however, you can plant hedging plants such as Olearia, Corokia, or Bottlebrush. Teucrium is also a great

Choosing the right roses for your garden

continued

choice; its grey leaves work well to enhance the colours of most roses. Hardy herbs such as rosemary are also ideal and practical as windbreaks — a sprig or two of rosemary makes a nice addition to chicken, fish or lamb cooked on the barbecue!

Any of the Rugosa group of roses or the China rose, Rosa mutablis (with honey-yellow flowers changing to pink and finally to red), are good repeat-flowerers and work well if you just want to plant and forget them. The Rugosas are possum resistant — great if you live in an isolated spot.

ROSES FOR CONTAINERS

Roses are ideal for containers provided you select the right size of container, but remember to deep water, feed and dead-head regularly. If using clay or terracotta containers remember they are porous, so paint the inside with a water-based paint or a similar preparation to reduce water loss.

MINIATURES

There is much satisfaction to be gained from some of the miniatures. I choose to grow all my miniature roses in containers. I find their diminutive features are shown to best advantage this way. Miniatures vary in size from those that grow 15cm to 90cm or more. Their flowers are small, usually in proportion to the size of the plant.

I use 20cm (8in) diameter terracotta pots as I have found they give the correct balance of moisture-retention

The Fairy, displayed in containers…

Trained as climbers...

Used as standards…

Simply added or mixed into the garden The Fairy always excites…

Choosing the right roses for your garden

continued

and aeration the roots need. Use a high-quality potting mix (tub and shrub mix) and apply a surface mulch of coarsely sieved garden compost or bark. Add a handful or two of water retention crystals such as Saturaid. When grouping miniatures in one pot, use a container of 45cm or more. Planting in odd numbers looks natural.

Water regularly during summer and feed twice a year. Container roses should be grown in full sun, but move them into light shade when they are in full flower to extend the life of the flowers. It is ideal to bring containers indoors when the roses are in flower. However, return them outdoors as soon as the flowers begin to fade. I always move them into a very lightly-shaded position as each flush of flowers finishes to harden them off before putting them back into the full sun.

Miniatures are ideal for use in hanging baskets. Three miniatures look stunning planted in the centre of a basket with a side planting of pansies or cascading petunias.

PATIO ROSES

Patio roses are medium-sized roses bred for container and garden use. Patio roses generally grow 90cm to a metre high. Their flowers are generally smaller than those of traditional roses. Standard patio roses, which are often grafted to 45cm stock, are ideal for container growing as they provide flowers at a good medium height.

Because of their size, patio roses are ideal for the smaller garden. Mini Pearl is a great performer. Glowing Touch and Lavender Lace also flower well. Little Flirt, with its loose flowers of red and yellow makes for a bright splash of colour in the garden and is a favourite. Wee Man, with red flowers and striking gold stamens is spectacular in the garden – ideal when planted in groups of three or more.

Choosing the right roses for your garden

continued

BILL'S HINT

For security why not plant the rose Climbing Mermaid. This free-flowering single golden gem has thorns that are quite impenetrable. A natural barrier, prowlers beware!

I have grown Sunmaid in a semi-shady position and was delighted with the results. To allow enough room for growth, plant in pots no smaller than 45cm across.

SHRUB ROSES

If opting for the larger-growing shrub such as the Hybrid Tea and David Austin roses, ensure you have a good-sized container. I recommend at least 90cm across. Some roses collapse in containers because the pot is not large enough to sustain the growth of the plant, resulting in its becoming pot-bound and starved.

Growing shrub roses on a frame or an obelisk in a pot is a novel idea. A good choice would be Abraham Darby; its big creamy apricot/yellow and fragrant blooms make it striking. Imagine two large black or green pots each with a black obelisk covered by a shrub rose such as Fair Bianca (a richly fragrant, milky white rose) framing an entrance – this would make a statement in style.

All container-grown roses need regular feeding. This is easily achieved by adding slow-release fertilisers such as Osmocote, Magamp or Debco rose booster; the latter has been developed to ensure maximum growth and flower potential.

Seasonal & successive planting for spectacular displays of colour

It is often said that roses are hungry plants which do not like having to compete for nutrients with other plants, trees or shrubs.

I, too, once believed this theory, but discovered by accident through planting some scilla bulbs under my roses that after the roses were pruned in early spring, the bulbs erupted into a shimmering blue display that looked quite enchanting.

Today one of the most challenging goals for gardeners is to keep colour in the garden. It is fine if you have a larger garden where you can devote separate areas to distinct seasonal effects. However, this is not the case for most of us. We need to plan for seasonal colour. With today's smaller gardens, it is not practical to leave parts of the garden inactive for long; you need to keep the whole garden working for you through the seasons.

I have learned by carefully selecting plants to grow with roses that I can achieve simultaneous and successive displays of flowers which provide year-round colour, rather than having to face roses blooming by themselves or worst of all, barren earth and the rather unsightly stark stems during the winter months.

PLANTS TO GROW THAT BLOOM WITH YOUR ROSES

It is easy to use annuals and perennials to achieve a simultaneous display of colour with roses forming part of the overall landscape.

ANNUALS

Plan ahead. This means you will have to plant three to four successive lots of seed to ensure blooms over the spring, summer and autumn when your roses are flowering. From seedling to flowering takes about eight weeks

Seasonal & successive planting for spectacular displays of colour

c o n t i n u e d

BILL'S TIP
Annuals need to be varied, as often they don't excel in the same spot year after year. If using annuals, plan for a seasonal change of plant.

and most flower displays last from six to 10 weeks. It requires some planning to get six to eight months of flowering displays from your annuals. However, potted seedlings are readily available from your garden supplier – a quick and easy alternative. Great for busy people!

The height of your annuals will be an issue if you have chosen larger roses or climbers. Annuals range in height from 10cm to 90cm, so depending on varieties they may not provide much relief from roses that are medium height upwards.

When you are planning to plant annuals with your roses, experiment with interesting colour combinations. Imagine bright yellow roses mixed with the butterfly-like white cosmos dancing in the breeze, bordered by sky-blue ageratum. How about a garden of blood-red roses mixed with creamy white Queen Anne lace and under-planted with ice pink or white

petunias — stunning!

I add larkspur and cosmos (for height) to my rose garden, mixed with begonias, petunias and ageratum. Planted in spring, they afford me at least five months display and can tolerate some drying out.

For easy-to-grow annuals look to the guide on page 24.

PERENNIALS

Depending on your site, consider staging your planting so you have a range of heights. For a taller cottage effect, use upright perennials such as hollyhock or delphinium. For a more formal look, choose just one variety of perennial. Formality is achieved by simplicity, not by mixing a multitude of plants. For medium height consider day lilies or Cranesbill geraniums, then under-plant with lavender, alyssum, pansies or the like. Imagine white roses mixed in with the bluey-purple Cranesbill geraniums — simple yet stylish. For a postcard

Seasonal & successive planting for spectacular displays of colour

continued

effect, imagine adding blue delphiniums and black hollyhocks edged with black viola to a white rose bed.

When using perennials, consider the height, colours and flowering times so that they complement rather than compete.

Climbers are particularly effective, but flower for a short period. They are spectacular, though, as their flowers are produced on the outer rims. Clematis (English hybrids) work well with climbers. Try adding the white perennial sweet pea (lyathrus) with the clematis as well. Lyathrus, an old-world sweet pea, gives a longer flowering period as well as a lovely fragrance.

I have recommended a range of successional flowering plants to be combined with roses and listed them into flowering times and colour groups. These are in the guide on pages 29.

BULBS

There are a number of summer-flowering bulbs that work well with roses. Rhodohypoxis, spraxias, ixias and alliums are some. Why not try a carpet of rhodohypoxis, lovely little bulbs that come in pink, white and red. They naturalise quickly, flower for a good three months and afford a gay display. Also refer to the guide on page 30.

PLANTS TO GROW THAT BLOOM AFTER YOUR ROSES

It is also easy to use annuals, bulbs and perennials to have successive or seasonal variety in garden beds and to avoid the starkness of the winter months after your roses have finished flowering.

ANNUALS

Annuals give quick relief when the garden is dormant. Annuals produce their blooms quicker than anything else and give you the widest range of colours. Successive plantings of annuals

Seasonal & successive planting for spectacular displays of colour

continued

give you colour all year round. Annuals are ideal in a mixed planting to fill in the gaps or for mass planting under roses to create a burst of colour. For winter why not liberally mix yellow or orange calendula into your garden and surround them with red or yellow polyanthus? This will lift your spirits even on the dullest of days. For a more formal look, under-plant with a mass of primula or pansy in your favourite colour. White always pleases. For a truly different look, ornamental kale is also worth considering.

A handy trick for a mixed border is to have some annuals coming on in containers or to simply buy a pot or two of potted colour and add these for instant colour. Seasonal varieties are readily available from your favourite garden supplier.

PERENNIALS

Perennials are useful as cover. However, many flower for a short period. Depend-ing on the situation, you may want tallish ground covers as a background. The campanula family of perennials range in height from 10cm to 45cm. Campanula is available in a colour range of purple, blue, white and pink. Another good choice is the hellebore, the 'winter rose'. Planted en masse, this wonderful plant provides welcome relief during the cold winter months.

Care needs to be taken with perennials. They will need thinning every second year to prevent them choking out other plants, including the roses. You should ensure the crown of the rose is kept free of growth as this can strangle and suffocate your rose bush.

Perennials such as nepeta (catnip or catmint) or alchimilla mollis (lady's mantle) are popular and commonly used. For something a little more imaginative, try adding a mass of cyclamen or euphorbia (particularly the euphorbia polychroma), which forms a

Seasonal & successive planting for spectacular displays of colour

continued

low mound with lime-yellow bract and lime-green leaves. Both perform well and are favourites of mine.

FOLIAGE PLANTS

Foliage can also be a useful component. Dark green bergenia (elephant's ear), black or green mondo grass, silver or golden lamb's ear, Stachus lanata, or grey liychnis all work well. In an open, sunny situation (ideal for the coast) the grey-leafed Artemisias "Powis Castle" are particularly stunning. Lavenders, native hebes and buxus are also good.

BULBS

Most winter and spring-flowering bulbs can be planted among roses and left to naturalise. The bulbs will form clumps that do not need to be disturbed unless flowering begins to fail.

It is advisable not to select varieties such as gladioli that need lifting each year as lifting disturbs the roots of roses, which may result in unwanted sucker growth.

In more formal gardens, avoid bulbs that have large straggly foliage which yellows and slowly dies after the flowering period. While this foliage may be gathered up and knotted to retain a neater appearance, (while still allowing it to die down naturally) it is still rather unsightly and can detract from the neat appearance of a more formal rose garden. Dutch iris are notorious for this.

Some suggestions for bulbs to use in formal gardens are crocus and dwarf narcissus; hyacinths are good if interplanted with violas, sweet william and the like. Try combining creamy freesias with yellowy orange lachenalias, or consider adding early cheer with blue muscaria – either combination will look fantastic if left to naturalise.

A useful tip – why not plant your bulbs in pots and then plant the pot in the garden? Once they have finished flowering lift them out and replant the spaces with potted colour of your choice.

A V A I L A B L E   C O L O U R S

Annuals	SEASON	ORANGE	RED	YELLOW	BLUE	WHITE	GREEN	CREAM	PINK	PURPLE
Ageratum	S				✽	✽			✽	
Alyssum	ALL YEAR		✽	✽	✽	✽		✽	✽	✽
Begonia	S	✽	✽			✽		✽	✽	
Candytuff	SP / S				✽	✽		✽	✽	✽
Dianthus	SP / S		✽			✽		✽	✽	
Celosia	S	✽	✽	✽				✽	✽	
Pyrethrum	S					✽				
Echium	S / A				✽				✽	
Californian Poppy	S / A	✽	✽	✽		✽		✽	✽	
Forget-me-not	W / S / A				✽	✽			✽	
Godetia	W / SP		✽			✽		✽	✽	✽
Honesty	W / SP					✽				✽
Petunia	S		✽	✽	✽	✽		✽	✽	✽
Pansy	ALL YEAR	✽	✽	✽	✽	✽		✽	✽	✽
Larkspur	W / SP		✽	✽	✽	✽		✽	✽	✽
Lobelia	ALL YEAR				✽	✽		✽	✽	✽
Lychnis	S / A		✽			✽			✽	
Marigold	S	✽	✽	✽		✽		✽		
Nemesia	SP / S / A	✽	✽	✽	✽	✽		✽	✽	
Nasturtium	ALL YEAR	✽	✽	✽		✽		✽		

From a traditional rose garden...

Why not combine plants to create fantastic displays while your roses flower?

Add plants to provide colour when your roses have
finished – the results are spectacular!

The perfect backdrop to outdoor living

SP = Spring
S = Summer
A = Autumn
W = Winter

Perennials

Perennials	SEASON	ORANGE	RED	YELLOW	BLUE	WHITE	GREEN	CREAM	PINK	PURPLE
Ajuga	SP / S				✿	✿			✿	✿
Achillea	S / A		✿	✿		✿		✿	✿	✿
Armaria (Thrift)	SP / A		✿			✿			✿	
Carnation	ALL YEAR	✿	✿	✿		✿		✿	✿	✿
Campanula	ALL YEAR				✿	✿		✿	✿	✿
Convolvulus	ALL YEAR				✿	✿				
Delphinium	SP / S		✿	✿	✿	✿		✿	✿	✿
Geum	ALL YEAR	✿	✿	✿				✿		
Hellebore	W / SP		✿			✿	✿	✿	✿	✿
Hollyhock	S		✿	✿		✿		✿	✿	✿
Hosta	SP / S					✿		✿		✿
Day Lily	ALL YEAR	✿	✿	✿		✿		✿	✿	✿
Lady's Mantle	ALL YEAR						✿			
Lavender	ALL YEAR				✿	✿	✿	✿	✿	✿
Monarda	S / A		✿		✿	✿			✿	✿
Pentstemon	SP / A		✿		✿	✿		✿	✿	✿
Rosemary	ALL YEAR				✿				✿	✿
Sage	ALL YEAR		✿		✿				✿	✿
Verbena	ALL YEAR		✿		✿	✿			✿	✿
Viola	ALL YEAR	✿	✿	✿	✿	✿		✿	✿	✿

Bulbs that flower with your roses

SP = Spring   S = Summer   A = Autumn   W = Winter

A V A I L A B L E   C O L O U R S

Bulbs	SEASON	ORANGE	RED	YELLOW	BLUE	WHITE	GREEN	CREAM	PINK	PURPLE
Beladonna	A					✿			✿	
Spraxia	S	✿	✿	✿		✿		✿	✿	✿
Ixia	S		✿			✿	✿	✿	✿	✿
Tulip	SP / S	✿	✿	✿		✿		✿	✿	✿
Trintonia					✿					
Lily	S	✿	✿	✿		✿		✿	✿	
Ranunculus	S	✿	✿	✿		✿	✿	✿	✿	
Iris	SP / S			✿	✿	✿				
Allium	S			✿						✿
Galtonia	S					✿	✿	✿		

Bulbs that flower after your roses

A V A I L A B L E   C O L O U R S

Bulbs	SEASON	ORANGE	RED	YELLOW	BLUE	WHITE	GREEN	CREAM	PINK	PURPLE
Anemone	SP		✿		✿	✿		✿	✿	✿
Freesia	SP / S		✿	✿	✿	✿		✿	✿	✿
Lachenalia	W	✿	✿	✿	✿		✿	✿		
Scilla	W				✿	✿				
Hyacinth	W			✿	✿	✿		✿	✿	✿
Daffodil	W / SP	✿		✿		✿		✿	✿	
Crocus	W / SP			✿	✿	✿				
Chionodoxa	W				✿	✿				
Ornithogalum (Star of Bethlehem)	W				✿	✿				
Camassia	W / SP				✿					✿

Making the most of roses

Most of us admire roses but do not use them effectively in our gardens. To make the most of roses read the following points and develop a plan to increase the number of roses in your garden.

Points to consider:

SITE, SPACE AND STRUCTURES

No matter how limited your space is, you can grow roses successfully. When considering adding a rose to your garden you may need to take a fresh look at the space available. As the years pass it is easy to become complacent and overlook many opportunities to plant this queen of flowers.

For example most homes have balconies, back doors, walls and fences which provide the ideal structures for growing roses.

Look around and identify sites that could provide a home for a climbing rose or two. Whether it is as a formal (reflected over a fence or brought up on chains to provide windows) or a more informal look (a single climber draped over a wall) climbing roses can create the most spectacular effect.

Roses can cover and disguise the most unsightly structures. They can soften hard lines and angles. Adding structures specifically on which to grow roses can enhance the dreariness of a dull wall, make an archway come alive or give height to an otherwise flat and

BILL'S TIP
Avoid growing roses through fruit trees — you may wish to climb to pick fruit. Also avoid choosing a dead or old tree. The weight of some climbers is enormous — it is not a pleasant task trying to untangle a tree with a rose in it after a gale has brought it down.

Making the most of roses

c o n t i n u e d

uninteresting area. Roses are amazingly versatile. You can easily train them to grow on almost anything, from rustic manuka frames, obelisks of wood or metal to poles and drainpipes. You will really enjoy the rewards gained from investing the time to grow and train a rose over such a structure.

Growing roses in containers is another area that is often overlooked. Most of us have a spare container or two about the house. These make ideal homes for roses (refer to roses in containers, pages 12–18 and the guide on pages 57–61) provided you choose the right type of rose, ensuring that it will thrive in the size of container available and that it is one which repeat-flowers freely.

Correctly under-planted containers of roses can provide a year-round display — add a few bulbs to your containers to provide interest in spring.

Standards can be rewarding. Reflected (using the same rose repetitively — photograph page 37), grouped or used in isolation they are quite fantastic. The Flower Carpet group excel when grafted to a standard. Red or pink Fairy and Seafoam are also well worth considering.

If you want to add some drama to your garden – reflect several weeping standards of the same rose — fantastic!

Making the most of roses

c o n t i n u e d

BILL'S HINT

When drying roses choose healthy specimens. Bend petals to the desired shape, dethorn while green, and hang them upside down in a cool, airy location. White roses are not recommended as they turn a muddy brown colour.

YOUR LIVING PATTERNS AND THE FLOW OF YOUR GARDEN

Plant your roses where you will get the most pleasure from them, and that will mean taking into account where you spend your time in the house and garden.

If you spend a lot of time indoors, plant your roses so they can be admired from where you sit. Window boxes or tall standards can be seen through your windows. Miniatures and Flower Carpets are ideal for window boxes. Lavender Lass, Iceberg and Freesia are good standards and well worth considering. Roses in containers can also be viewed from living room windows.

If you are like me and you like to spend time outdoors, why not set up a screen or perhaps a wooden or metal framework over your patio or outdoor area. You could create your own "rose room" — an ideal extension to the house.

Consider how you move around your garden. This is known as the "flow". Think about planting roses for colour or fragrance at points where you regularly come into contact with them rather than tucking them away.

THE IMPORTANCE OF FRAGRANCE.

I once heard a description of the fragrance of a rose grown by an entrance as one of the best "welcome homes". Having incorporated this idea into my own patch, I find it hard to resist the

Making the most of roses

continued

BILL'S HINT

GRANDMA'S REMEDY – Pick your roses early in the day. Once indoors, recut the stems on a 45-degree angle. Put the stems into boiling water for one minute then plunge them into cold water. Remove all leaves that will be under water in the vase. Add a teaspoon of sugar and a drop of Janola to the vase water. Place the flowers in a cool spot.

seductively sweet fragrance of Madame Alfred Carriere.

Repeat-flowering fragrant roses that I have used in my garden include: Just Joey — sweet yet not overpowering; Freesia, soft and lingering and as the name suggests very similar to the smell of the popular freesia flowers we enjoy in spring; Madame Isaac Pereire would have to be the most intensely fragrant of all, generous in its flowers and flamboyant in its perfume — a single bloom will fragrance a room.

A more detailed list of repeat-flowering, fragrant roses is at the back of this book.

ROSES FOR PICKING

If you have space for only a few roses, you should ensure they are types that work well both in the garden and indoors, as a cut flower.

Roses are perhaps the most romantic flowers — they can enhance any mood. Although relatively short-lived (in terms of vase life), if chosen correctly the colour and/or scent provide a real treat. I love picking roses and some of my favourites for the vase are Royal William, Playboy and Paddy Stevens. Every year a friend brings me an enormous bunch of Aotearoa (lovely

Making the most of roses

continued

pinky white flowers). They last for what seems like ages and always draw favourable comments from my guests.

Some roses hold their blooms better than others. Those that last well are often the result of specific breeding aimed at achieving this result. I have listed in my guide at the end of this book the roses that flower well on the bush and at the same time work well as cut flowers — the majority having fragrance as a bonus.

PLANTING ROSES – CONSIDERATIONS OF COLOUR AND LIGHT

Colour — nothing in a garden makes more impact! Colour can stop you in your tracks or beckon you onwards. It can suggest coolness and warmth or evoke different moods such as intimacy or, dare I say, even seduction... there is nothing more romantic than a rose.

Dedicated rose beds, often in a multitude of colours, were once in vogue. Today, however, we are more interested in the use of colour to create and manipulate the look, space and feel of the garden. By combining roses and flower/foliage colours of other plants we are able to create harmonies, contrasts or clashes of colour.

Harmonies occur if the colours of the plants are similar or different shades of one colour. Combining roses such as Elina, Dimples and City of Auckland provides for a harmony of creamy lemon and buff yellow where the colours blend and merge successfully.

Contrasts are where two or more colours are placed together so that the colours chosen intensify one another — pinks and whites, reds and creams. When contrasts of colour are used they create a sense of closeness and intimacy — such combinations are ideal for patio areas, entrances and the like.

Clashes occur when the colours chosen fight one another — reds

Making the most of roses

continued

combined with pinks, oranges with purples. Such colour combinations will stop you in your tracks and are best used where you wish to stop the flow and create a sense of "wow"! Clashes of colour generally need to be admired from a distance. If your garden space is limited, using clashes can be quite overpowering as they tend to dominate.

The way to use colour through roses and associated plantings is as personal to you as the decoration of your house. There are no rights or wrongs. However, if you want to create a stunning display by controlling your colours you must decide on a colour scheme for each area of your garden or for your garden overall. If you like pastels, stay with pastels; if it is to be primary colours, stay with them.

Once you have chosen your scheme you must discipline yourself to use only those plants with flowers and foliage that works within this colour range in each season. Too often we are fooled into adding plants that don't work because we picked them up at a sale, on impulse or because they were a gift. Adding plants with colours that don't work is to be avoided.

Remember you do not need to rely on flowers alone for all-year colour. Foliage provides colour over a longer period and changes with the seasons. For a permanent feature try adding some plants with silver or grey foliage, such as Artemisia or lavender. This combination works beautifully with roses.

Reflected

Roses in window boxes. Looking in...

Looking out...

Displayed in containers. Roses can be added almost anywhere.

Making the most of roses

c o n t i n u e d

If you are unsure what scheme is right for you (harmonies, contrasts or clashes) I recommend you start with a single colour. Once this is done you can build on your colour choice simply by adding and combining variations of the colour you have chosen.

THE USE OF LIGHT

Effective use of light in the garden is a field of study in itself. Here are some fundamentals of using light for the average gardener to consider:

In areas bathed by sunlight, the hot flower colours such as reds, oranges, and yellows work well. These colours are ideal for use in areas frequented during the day. A fabulous effect can be created if you plan your plantings so that these colours can be viewed regularly from the main living areas such as the kitchen or dining room. Using too much white in these situations can be a bit glary.

However, white is ideal if you wish to make a statement, so use it in or alongside an entrance, or as a border. It is also effective if you are nocturnal in your habits and like to entertain or enjoy your garden after dark. Whites work well in this situation as they remain visible well into the night.

Planning your planting

In summary to create a successful garden using roses you need to consider:

- The site — particularly the sun aspect, drainage, watering requirements and air flow.
- Structures available now or that you intend to add to support your roses.
- Colours that you enjoy and the effect those colours create.
- The flow of the space/garden and how you plan to use the garden.
- Formal versus informal planting styles.
- Selecting the right roses for you and your garden so that you have the most flowers for the longest time.
- What seasonal and successive plants you need to add to provide year-round colour and interest - bulbs, annuals, perennials or flowering trees or shrubs.

ADDING ROSES TO YOUR EXISTING GARDEN

For some of us, our gardens whilst established, are still a disappointment. If this is you and you want to create excitement and colour with roses, then read on.

Select your site and remove any material past its best or which does not work with the existing plantings. Prune all diseased, spent or damaged plant material, weed and tidy the area. Dig over the ground deeply. Add a good dressing of a general fertiliser or organic manure at 150 grams per square metre. Depending upon soil type, add peat, mushroom compost or your own compost to a depth of 10cm. Work everything in well. Leave for a few days.

This is the ideal time to add a watering system.

Select one or two of your favourite repeat-flowering rose varieties that will suit the site and plant away. Remember

Planning your planting

continued

when choosing your roses to take into account the colour effects of any trees or shrubs that may flower during the same period. Plant your roses 1–1.5 metres apart to allow good air movement.

Consider roses such as the Flower Carpets and miniatures for areas requiring low-growing plants. Roses such as the Hybrid Tea, Floribunda, English and the Austin's are ideal for those areas that need something larger. Depending on type they will grow 1–1.5 metres tall. Ensure you plant these roses outside the drip line of any large plants or trees you may have.

If you want to plant roses to climb trees, plant them well inside the drip line otherwise they will compete with the tree for food. Once planted, ensure you feed and water your climbers regularly as inside the drip line of a large tree is often the driest area in a garden.

If you already have a mixture of colours and textures in your garden I recommend you choose a rose colour to complement rather than compete — cream, white or lemon are always good choices. These colours tend to soften and give depth to otherwise uninteresting areas.

PLANNING & PLANTING A NEW GARDEN

When planning a new garden consider using roses as the framework.

Roses grouped in clusters, singly staged or reflected, or even planted as a hedge will create a flower display that will out-perform any other.

For an informal spring look, add into this mix foxgloves, shrubby clematis, lupin and others. A mixed perennial border with roses looks great – in fact it can be really stunning.

In a one-sided bed, select taller plants such as hollyhock, delphinium or Queen Anne lace for the background. Intersperse with your favourite summer

Planning your planting

continued

flowering annuals through the mid and foreground areas. A list of suitable annuals is provided on page 24.

Consider adding interesting foliage for texture and combine with other plants to provide interest and variation; for example, the grey and silver foliage of astelias, which have flax-like leaves, and artemisia, whose ferny, lace-like leaves provide a sense of drama in any colour combination.

There are many plants that can be combined to create whatever look you fancy.

Formality with roses is achieved through similarity in planting, either pairing — for example, the same rose in pots on either side of an entrance — or reflecting a planting — that is, having four or five containers of one rose placed evenly down a drive or along a decking.

PLANTING YOUR ROSES

Here are a few general guidelines for planting your roses:

Thoroughly water your rose before planting. Dig the hole a little deeper than the bag the rose is in and twice as wide. The bud union on the rose should be level with or slightly above the ground. Mix into the hole a little slow-release fertiliser or several handfuls of fowl or sheep manure. Remove your plant from its bag or container and inspect the plant for any broken roots or stems — cut these off. Place the root ball into the hole and carefully firm in the soil around the root area until the hole is half full. Add more sheep pellets and fill in the hole. Water well.

Caring for your roses

BILL'S HINT

If your roses flowerheads droop early after picking, recut and place the bottom of the stems in boiling water for a minute. Then place them into cool water. Put a pin all the way through each stem just under the bloom — this allows the trapped air to escape. This air has been keeping water from the bloom. Keep in a cool place.

The following are tips on how to care for your roses:

SUN

Most roses need sunshine and plenty of it. The minimum requirement for most roses is five hours a day. Such roses, if grown in full sun, are less susceptible to disease and will bloom well and for longer than the same rose which has been forced to eke out an existence in the shade. There are however some roses that thrive in shady situations — refer to pages 57–61.

SOIL

Heavy soil is ideal for roses as it retains water. If your soil is light you will need a lot of compost. All soils should be dug well and have generous amounts of peat and compost. A light dressing of lime or dolomite is also beneficial at this time.

For a new bed I recommend adding a compost mulch to a depth of about 8cm around your plant as this will help to retain moisture during the hot summer months, particularly if you do not intend to under-plant. Pea straw is an ideal mulch and it reduces weed growth as well.

AIR

Your rose plants must have air circulating around and through them. This will help to ensure the risk of fungal infection is reduced during humid weather.

Caring for your roses

c o n t i n u e d

BILL'S HINT

When flowers begin to wither, you need to remove them. This is called deadheading. Removing the spent flowers encourages more flowers to develop and reduces the risk of fungal infections.

DRAINAGE AND WATERING

While roses are tolerant of most things, they do not like wet feet. Ensure you choose a well-drained position for your plants. A raised bed is best. This can be achieved by mounding up the existing soil and adding compost, peat and extra soil. Aim to raise the soil level by 15-20 cm. Ensure you mix all the materials thoroughly.

SHELTER

If you want to plant your roses in an open situation you need some shelter.

Roses are prone to wind damage. Try to provide some form of windbreak (trellis, or shelter belt) and ensure you stake the roses securely. Many commercial stakes are available — wood, metal and bamboo are ideal. Position stakes 20-30 cm from the trunk of the rose. This will ensure you avoid the root ball of your plant. Tie in a figure eight using soft material such as pantyhose, strips of rubber or old hose pieces. Garden

supply shops have different proprietary brands of ties available. Never use wire as it will cut into your prized rose, ring-barking it and causing it to die.

FERTILISING AND FEEDING YOUR ROSES

When you plant your roses add one of the slow-release fertilisers. This will continue to feed your plants for some months. Additional top dressings should be applied four times a year. Apply the first dressing in early spring, the second with the spring flush, again in late summer and finally, early autumn. A handful of fertiliser per square metre around your plants is sufficient.

Caring for your roses

c o n t i n u e d

WHAT TO FEED YOUR ROSES

NUTRIENTS

The most important nutrients for roses are nitrogen, phosphorus and potassium in a mix of 8:4:10 respectively. Fowl manure is the closest natural mix to this ratio for your roses. Cow manure and sheep pellets are good second choices.

TRACE ELEMENTS

Calcium and iron found in blood and bone and magnesium and boron found in fish meal are also vital for the health of your roses.

For Easy Care I recommend:

Plenty of aged fowl manure applied during the first signs of growth then every 6–8 weeks apply a generous mix of blood and bone and fish meal until late summer. Debco Rose Booster does it all.

For that Picture Postcard display:

Following is the feeding regime used for one of the best award-winning displays of roses I have ever seen:

- Apply sheep pellets liberally in August (try well-rotted fowl manure if you can get it).
- Four weeks later add a handful of Nitrophoska Blue every square metre.
- Fish Fertiliser Moana (as a liquid foliage feed every 10 days) – the leaves take up the nutrients and then translocate them to all parts of the plants — try to avoid spraying if you have guests arriving — no need to say why!
- October, December, February and March apply a liberal dressing of blood and bone.

A sign of insufficient fertiliser is stunted growth and irregularly coloured leaves on your roses.

WATER

Water is the most important element to successful rose growing. Water needs to be applied generously before and after

Caring for your roses

continued

feeding, mulching and during the growing period.

Water carries the nutrients in the fertilisers to the growing roots of your roses, creating healthy plants.

As a general guide during a normal summer (not drought) you need to deep water your roses, this means about half an hour of watering every three to four days for each established rose. This is easily achieved for those lazy gardeners among us by installing a Plassay drip system.

A splash-and-dash watering with the hose on alternative warm summer evenings in between a gin or two will not do. In fact you do more damage than good, as this type of approach encourages the feeder roots to grow in the top few centimetres of soil where they will dry out. If roots dry out too often the plant becomes stunted, straggly and prone to disease.

Light watering is one of the main reasons many rose growers have little success. Regular watering will eliminate disappointment.

PRUNING

For successful flowering each season roses need to be pruned. There are many good books on the subject. For more information contact your local garden centre. Some garden centres have regular pruning demonstrations which are worth attending.

Flowercarpet Roses form the framework of these gardens.

before

In just three years — transformation

before

Side fence removed, entrance way added and then framed in roses.

Iceberg roses added to this home creates
a more formal look – works well.

Common pests & diseases

BILL'S HINT
Sprays don't work in wet or windy conditions. Spray your chemicals directly on the dry leaves and ensure the forecast is for at least four to five hours of clear weather. It is best to spray in the early morning when the air is still.

Listed below are some of the most common pests and diseases and ways in which you can eliminate them:

APHIDS

These are small, usually green or reddish black/brownish insects that live in colonies. They are usually found in vast quantities on new shoots—spring to autumn. They suck out the sap of the plants, causing distortion of the leaves and flowers. They are easily controlled with carbaryl or malathion. A soapy solution sprayed on the infected area will also work well.

BLACKSPOT

Prevalent on roses when humidity is high. Recognisable when leaves start to exhibit black or purply-brown spots. If left untreated the leaf yellows and dies. Spray with super copper (copperoxychloride) at 10-day intervals.

DOWNY MILDEW

If you find a furry growth on the underside of your rose leaves then it is likely to be downy mildew. A common problem in the cool moist conditions of early spring and autumn. I suggest using Bravo or Shield.

MITES

Most commonly found in hot, dry conditions. Mites are barely visible to the naked eye but they can cause yellowing of leaves and severe leaf drop. Use Mavrik every three to five days.

POWDERY MILDEW

A grey-white, dust-like substance on the tops of leaves, stems or flower heads. You can spray to control this with a specific mildew chemical, or dust flowers with sulphur if the infection is localised. Cut out and discard (burn or take to the tip — do not put into your compost as the disease will spread) any foliage or flowers from your affected plants.

Common pests & diseases

continued

THRIPS

Thrips turn your rose leaves silver and leave the flower petals brown. Thrips also attack the rose buds, leaving them deformed and blackening petal edges. Thrips can be quite hard to get rid of, so spray every three to five days with Confidor. Generally it takes three to four sprays to eliminate this pest.

RUST

Rust is often seen on roses and is identifiable by yellow spots on the top of the leaves with orangey-yellow pustules on the underside. Leaves may fall prematurely. Predominantly a dry-weather disease. Remove affected leaves and burn. Dust with sulphur or spray with a broad-spectrum fungicide.

SCALE

Identified as hard scale-like insects on stems and canes. Spray with an oil such as Conqueror, adding Malathion or Orthene.

SILVER LEAF

This is a nasty problem and can be identified easily as the leaves of your rose actually turn silver and plant growth is usually stunted. The best way to control this is to dig out the plant and replace it. If you want to try to save your plant, cut all the infected area out and burn the discarded material. Ensure you sterilise your pruning equipment after pruning.

Answers to the most commonly asked questions

Q *How often do you repot roses grown in containers?*

A Every two years.

Q *Is there an organic spraying method for powdery mildew on roses?*

A Yes — baking soda. Two table-spoons dissolved in 4.5 litres of water sprayed every five days where infection is obvious.

Q *When can I shift my roses?*

A Winter is best, but they can be shifted all year round. If you are moving them during the growing season cut them back hard (by at least two-thirds).

Q *Can roses be grown from cuttings?*

A Yes. The best time to take cuttings is in January/February. Use a semi-hardwood cutting of around 15–20cm in length, cutting the base at a leaf node (ensure you have at least three pairs of buds on the cutting). Dip the cutting into a rooting hormone to help promote root growth. A third of the cutting should be placed into a coarse soil mix, leaving two nodes above the ground. Keep well watered.

Q *Some of my rose flowers lose colour - why?*

A This is a sulphate of potash deficiency. Potash is the essential element for flowering and fruiting. To remedy, apply a light dressing (handful) in early summer and again in early autumn. Water well.

Q *The buds of my roses are distorted?*

A Generally bud distortion is caused by insect damage. Identify the insect and spray with a general insecticide. Why not go organic and use a pyrethrum and garlic spray.

Q *My container roses have lost all their leaves?*

A Stress is the most likely cause - the roses being either too dry or too wet. (Check the type of rose and size of container required — refer to pages 12–18 and 57–61 on roses for containers.)

Answers to the most commonly asked questions

continued

Q *Are there any good repeating thornless roses I can grow?*

A Yes. Crepuscule and Madame Alfred Carriere are two I recommend.

Q *Why do my roses develop pink marks or spots on the petals?*

A This problem is due to water on the petals when the sun hits them. Avoid watering during the day.

Q *If I want a flush of roses, how long from pruning must I wait?*

A Generally 10–13 weeks.

Q *What are the best rose choices to grow through trees?*

A If you want a cream rose, Alberic Barbier would be my choice. Rambling Rector (red) is also very good.

Q *What is the difference between a climber and a rambler?*

A Climbers need training and flower on the horizontal canes. They seldom exceed six metres - ideal for the home garden. Ramblers are more vigorous and will cover up to 10 metres or more.

Q *Roses for hedges - suggestions please?*

A Sally Holmes, The Fairy, Iceberg and all the Rugosas are an excellent selection.

Q *Can I use liquid plant food around my roses?*

A Yes – fish, seaweed and balanced commercial preparations are all beneficial. Don't use the same one all year. They are great as a supplement.

Q *My roses produce lush foliage with little flowering - why?*

A I believe the cause is nutritional. Your ground is probably too high in nitrogen, which will produce healthy leaf growth but little in the way of flowers. Roses require a more balanced fertiliser. I suggest you add potash.

A list of repeat-flowering roses that excel

Whites

	COLOUR	TYPE	FRAGRANT	REPEAT	PERPETUAL CONTINUOUS	GREAT FOR PICKING	SHADE TOLERANT	SEA/SALT TOLERANT	IDEAL FOR CONTAINERS	IDEAL FOR BASKETS	GOOD GARDEN ROSE	CLIMBERS
Aotearoa	Pinky White	Hybrid tea	❀	❀		❀	❀		❀		❀	
Pascali	Cream White	Hybrid tea	❀	❀		❀	❀		❀		❀	
Mrs Herbert Stevens	White	Floribunda	❀		❀	❀	❀				❀	
Margaret Merril	White	Floribunda	❀	❀		❀	❀		❀		❀	
Iceberg	Flat White	Floribunda		❀		❀	❀	❀	❀		❀	
Auckland Metro	Light White	Floribunda	❀	❀		❀	❀		❀		❀	
Avalanche	Pure White	Floribunda		❀		❀	❀	❀	❀		❀	
Remuera	Clear White	Floribunda	❀	❀		❀	❀		❀		❀	
Little Scotch	Creamy White	Miniature			❀		❀	❀	❀		❀	
Fair Bianca	White	English*	❀	❀		❀	❀				❀	
Dove	White	English*	❀	❀		❀	❀				❀	
Swan	White	English*	❀	❀		❀	❀				❀	
Blanc double de Coubert	White	Old World	❀		❀	❀	❀				❀	
Prosperity	White	Old World	❀		❀	❀	❀	❀			❀	
Bride	White	Old World		❀		❀					❀	
Mdme Alfred Carriere	White	Climbing	❀	❀		❀	❀	❀			❀	❀
Pax	White	Climbing		❀				❀			❀	❀
Seafoam	White	Climbing			❀	❀	❀	❀			❀	❀
Snow Carpet	White	Miniature		❀					❀		❀	
White Flower Carpet	White	Miniature			❀					❀	❀	
Penelope	White	Old World	❀	❀		❀					❀	

*David Austin

57

Unusual

	COLOUR	TYPE	FRAGRANT	REPEAT	PERPETUAL CONTINUOUS	GREAT FOR PICKING	SHADE TOLERANT	SEA/SALT TOLERANT	IDEAL FOR CONTAINERS	IDEAL FOR BASKETS	GOOD GARDEN ROSE	CLIMBERS
Mutabilis	Pink/Yellow Red	Old World			✿				✿		✿	
Hot Chocolate	Russet Brown	Floribunda	✿			✿					✿	
Double Delight	Cream/Red	Floribunda	✿			✿			✿		✿	
Handel	Cream/Rose pink	Climber	✿			✿					✿	✿
Lydia	Gay mix red & yel	Climber	✿			✿			✿		✿	✿
Royal Lavender	Lav Grey Pink	Climber	✿			✿					✿	✿
Hansa	Reddish Purple	Old World	✿			✿					✿	
Lavender Lassie	Lavender Pink	Old World	✿			✿			✿		✿	
Old Port	Burgundy Purple	Miniature	✿			✿			✿		✿	
Ripples	Lavender	Floribunda	✿	✿		✿					✿	
Lilac Rose	Lavender	English*	✿	✿		✿	✿	✿			✿	
Red												
Alexander	Red/Orange	Hybrid tea	✿	✿		✿					✿	
Deep Secret	Dark Red	Hybrid tea	✿	✿		✿					✿	
Erotica	Velvet Crimson	Hybrid tea	✿	✿		✿					✿	
Fragrant Cloud	Tomato	Hybrid tea	✿	✿		✿					✿	
Lady in Red	Velvet Red	Hybrid tea	✿	✿		✿					✿	
Royal William	Deep Red	Hybrid tea	✿	✿		✿					✿	
Black Jade	Black Red	Miniature	✿	✿		✿			✿		✿	
Kaikoura	Scarlet Red	Miniature		✿		✿			✿		✿	
Patio Prince	Dark Red	Miniature		✿					✿		✿	
Eye Opener	Deep Red	Miniature		✿					✿	✿	✿	

*David Austin

	COLOUR	TYPE	FRAGRANT	REPEAT	PERPETUAL CONTINUOUS	GREAT FOR PICKING	SHADE TOLERANT	SEA/SALT TOLERANT	IDEAL FOR CONTAINERS	IDEAL FOR BASKETS	GOOD GARDEN ROSE	CLIMBERS
Red Fairy	Red	Miniature		✽		✽			✽	✽	✽	
Robin Redbreast	Red	Miniature		✽					✽	✽	✽	✽
Dublin Bay	Deep Red	Climber	✽	✽		✽					✽	✽
Etoile de Hollande	Dark Red	Climber	✽	✽		✽					✽	✽
Ena Harkness	Velvet Crimson	Climber	✽	✽		✽					✽	✽
Nancy Hayward	Cherry Red	Climber		✽		✽		✽			✽	✽
Mrs Anthony Waterer	Rich Crimson	Old World			✽	✽					✽	
Othello	Dark Crimson	English*	✽	✽		✽					✽	
Prospero	Dark Crimson	English*	✽	✽		✽					✽	
The Squire	Dark Crimson	English*	✽	✽		✽					✽	
William Shakespeare	Deep Red	English*		✽		✽					✽	
Colour Break	Red	Floribunda	✽	✽		✽			✽		✽	
Frensham	Red	Floribunda		✽		✽		✽	✽		✽	
Hans Christian Anderson	Red	Floribunda	✽	✽		✽		✽	✽		✽	
Trumpeter	Red	Floribunda	✽	✽		✽					✽	
Apricot												
Just Joey	Apricot Orange	Hybrid tea	✽	✽		✽					✽	
Julia's Rose	Coppery	Hybrid tea		✽		✽			✽		✽	
Play Boy	Coppery	Hybrid tea		✽		✽	✽	✽	✽		✽	
Perle d'Or	Coppery	Old World		✽		✽	✽	✽	✽		✽	
French Lace	Ivory Apricot	Floribunda	✽	✽		✽	✽	✽	✽		✽	
Matangi	Orange	Floribunda		✽		✽		✽	✽		✽	

*David Austin

Apricot (CONTINUED)	COLOUR	TYPE	FRAGRANT	REPEAT	PERPETUAL CONTINUOUS	GREAT FOR PICKING	SHADE TOLERANT	SEA/SALT TOLERANT	IDEAL FOR CONTAINERS	IDEAL FOR BASKETS	GOOD GARDEN ROSE	CLIMBERS
Schoolgirl	Ochre Apricot	Minature		❀		❀		❀			❀	❀
Westerland	Salmon Apricot	Climber		❀		❀					❀	❀
Crepuscule	Rich Apricot	Climber		❀	❀	❀		❀			❀	❀
Perdita	Soft Apricot	English*	❀	❀	❀	❀					❀	
Abraham Darby	Yellow Apricot	English*	❀	❀		❀					❀	
Yellow												
City of Auckland	Gold	Hybrid tea	❀			❀		❀	❀		❀	
Elina	Creamy Yellow	Hybrid tea	❀			❀	❀	❀			❀	
Sutter's Gold	Golden Yellow	Hybrid tea	❀			❀					❀	
Dimples	Lemon Yellow	Floribunda	❀			❀					❀	
Apricot Nectar	Buff Yellow	Floribunda	❀			❀			❀		❀	
Friesia	Bright Yellow	Floribunda	❀			❀			❀		❀	
Sequoia Gold	Bright Gold	Miniature	❀			❀			❀		❀	
Yellow Carpet Flower	Butter Yellow	Miniature			❀			❀	❀	❀	❀	
Graham Thomas	Rich Yellow	English*	❀			❀					❀	
Sweet Juliet	Apricot Yellow	English*	❀			❀					❀	
Windrush	Lemon Yellow	English*	❀		❀	❀	❀	❀			❀	
Golden Showers	Deep Gold Yellow	Climber	❀		❀	❀	❀	❀			❀	❀
Lady Hillingdon	Rich Yellow	Climber	❀	❀		❀					❀	❀
Agnes	Creamy Yellow	Old World	❀	❀		❀			❀		❀	
Buff Beauty	Apricot Yellow	Old World	❀	❀		❀					❀	
Celine Forestier	Peachy Yellow	Old World	❀	❀		❀					❀	
Butterflies	Glowing Yellow	Old World	❀	❀		❀					❀	

*David Austin

Pink

	COLOUR	TYPE	FRAGRANT	REPEAT	PERPETUAL CONTINUOUS	GREAT FOR PICKING	SHADE TOLERANT	SEA/SALT TOLERANT	IDEAL FOR CONTAINERS	IDEAL FOR BASKETS	GOOD GARDEN ROSE	CLIMBERS
Aotearoa	Pinky White	Hybrid tea	✿	✿		✿	✿		✿		✿	
Paddy Stevens	Coral Salmon	Hybrid tea	✿	✿		✿			✿		✿	
Carolyn	Clear Pink	Hybrid tea	✿	✿		✿					✿	
Pania	Buff Pink	Hybrid tea	✿	✿		✿					✿	
Fairy Dancer	Rose Pink	Floribunda		✿		✿			✿		✿	
Sexy Rexy	Delicate Pink	Floribunda	✿	✿		✿			✿		✿	
Spiced Coffee	Amber Pink	Floribunda	✿	✿		✿			✿		✿	
Julian McGredy	Gentle Pink	Floribunda	✿	✿		✿					✿	
Mini Pearl	Creamy Pink	Miniature	✿	✿		✿			✿		✿	
Constance Spry	Pale Pink	English*			✿		✿				✿	
Heritage	Light Pink	English*	✿	✿		✿			✿		✿	
Mary Rose	Rich Pink	English*	✿	✿		✿					✿	
Gertrude Jekyll	Rich Pink	English*	✿	✿		✿					✿	
The Friar	Blush Pink	English*	✿	✿		✿					✿	
Wife of Bath	Pastel Pink	English*	✿	✿		✿					✿	
Bloomfield Abundance	Creamy Pink	Climber			✿	✿	✿	✿			✿	✿
Bantry Bay	Medium Pink	Climber		✿		✿					✿	✿
New Dawn	Soft Pink	Climber			✿		✿	✿	✿		✿	✿
Shot Silk	Cloud Pink	Climber	✿	✿		✿					✿	✿

*David Austin

Thanks

Thanks to the staff of Business Coaching New Zealand, especially Ruth and Mark for their ongoing support and encouragement. A special thanks also to Margaret for her time and energy in editing this text. Thanks to Peg from Greens Garden Centre in Hamilton for her innovative ideas and continued support.

To my "Piglet" — thank you for your constant support and never-ending love.

Bill Uses

Rose Booster and Green Jacket slow-release fertiliser

Gardening trowels from the Campbell Tool Company – great products that really stand the test of time.

Hanging Baskets – Just Moss instant sphagnum moss liners and prepared "combo" packs are a truly great idea, ideal for all my hanging baskets.

Window boxes from Cottage Iron Works Ltd – these wrought iron boxes are a quality product, rust-proofed and available in a great range of colours and styles. They add a touch of style to even the most discerning gardener's home. For more information contact PO Box 13-131 Onehunga for your local stockist.

Plastic pots from Europots – these lightweight pots look great both in and out of doors and are available through all leading garden centres.

Homemade glazed pots from Morris and James – brighten up your home with these.

Osmocote Fertiliser – generously mix this fertiliser with your soil as you plant up your beds, baskets and window boxes.

Saturaid – rewetting granules – mix these in generously when planting to help to retain moisture in your baskets and window boxes.

Maxicrop Fertiliser – apply every two to three weeks when your plants are growing and flowering.

Plassay Watering System from Yates – keeps my plants healthy and well watered during even the driest summers.

Yates Pyrethrum and Conqueror – these are great general insecticides and Copperoxychloride is good as a general fungicide spray.

Notes

Notes